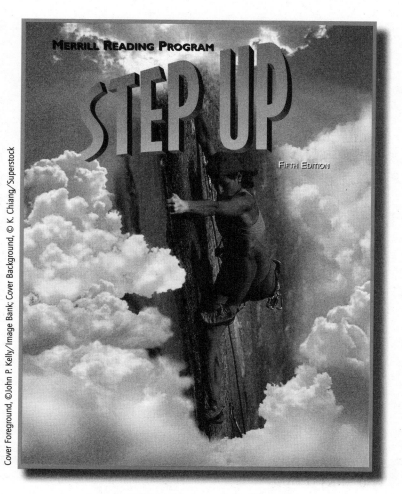

Cover Foreground, ©John P. Kelly/Image Bank; Cover Background, © K. Chiang/Superstock

MERRILL READING PROGRAM

STEP UP

FIFTH EDITION

Based on the philosophy of Charles C. Fries

Authors

Phyllis Bertin
Educational Coordinator
Windward School
White Plains, New York

Dr. Cecil D. Mercer
Professor of Education
University of Florida
Gainesville, Florida

Eileen Perlman
Learning Disabilities Specialist
White Plains Public Schools
White Plains, New York

Mildred K. Rudolph

Rosemary G. Wilson

 **SRA McGraw-Hill**

Columbus, Ohio

A Division of The **McGraw·Hill** *Companies*

TABLE OF CONTENTS

A Good Plan 6

Good, Better, Best 8

Plums for Lunch. 9

Rags and Dr. Miller 12

School in September 14

Time, Time, Time 16

Ted 18

At Pam's House 20

At the Letter Box 24

Sledding 26

Who Will Go Sledding? 28

The School Flag 30

After School 32

A Map 36

Ms. King's Gift 38

Spelling, Plants, and Bugs 41

The Puppy and the Top 44

The Inky Puppy 46

You Can Do This 48

What Can We Do? 50

Lots of Stems 52

Let's Look It Up 54

SRA/McGraw-Hill

A Division of The McGraw-Hill Companies

Copyright © 1999 by SRA/McGraw-Hill. All rights reserved. Except as permitted under the United States Copyright Act, no part of this publication may be reproduced or distributed in any form or by any means, or stored in a database or retrieval system, without prior written permission from the publisher.

Printed in the United States of America.

Send all inquiries to:
SRA/McGraw-Hill
8787 Orion Place
Columbus, Ohio 43240-4027

ISBN 0-02-674711-1

2 3 4 5 6 7 8 9 RRC 02 01 00

At Peg's Plant Shop 56

Good Luck for Pam 58

They Say "Stop" 60

The Pet Shop 62

Swing or Swim? 66

Picking a Swing 68

A Pet in the Woods 72

A Log Cabin 74

You Can Do It 76

To Catch a Crab 78

May I Help? 80

Catching a Frog 84

Look It Up 88

Not a Drop To Drink 90

A Wet Day at Home 92

Linda's Gift 96

A House for Sandy 98

Planning a Trip 102

Lucky, the Ranch Horse 105

To the Teacher 108

plan

plant

plum

plump

what

man	pan	gum	plant
pan	plan	hum	plum
plan	plant	plum	plump

A Good Plan

On a sunny day, Tom said to Dot, "I have a plan for today. I think I will dig a pit to set this plant in. Then when the plant gets big, we can have the plums from it."

"What a good plan, Tom!" said Dot. "I'll help you dig. Let's plant it next to the kitchen."

"Yes," said Tom, "let's get going."

When Tom bent to dig, he said, "Dot, I must be getting plump. I can't bend much to do this digging."

"That's OK," said Dot, "we'll get it dug."

Just then Tom yelled, "I've cut my hand!"

Dot rushed Tom to the doctor. The doctor fixed the cut and then said, "Mr. Bell, your hand will get better. But you will have to rest today."

On the way home, Dot said, "What a day! Your plan was good. You just had a little bad luck. Dan and Jan can dig the pit and set the plant in it for us."

At dinner Tom said to Dan and Jan, "You did a good job. But what a fuss for a little plum plant!"

Good, Better, Best

Dan and Jan did a good job when they dug the pit for Mom and Dad's plant. Mom and Dad hugged them, and Mom said, "You did such a good job with the plant that I have made up a song for you."

Here is Mom's song.

> I did a good job.
> Then I did it better.
> At last, I did it best.
>
> My mom said to me,
> "Good, better, best,
> Do not let it rest
> Till the good is better
> And the better is best!"

Plums for Lunch

After Dan and Jan had set the plant in the pit by the kitchen, they kept looking to see if it got bigger. Day after day they ran home from school to check on the plant. But the plant didn't look bigger to them.

Then on a very hot, sunny day Jan went to look at the plant. It looked bigger to her. She ran to get Dan.

"Dan," she yelled, "what do you think? Look at the plant! It looks so much bigger!"

Dan went with Jan to look at the plant. Then he said, "We have looked at it so much we didn't see it getting bigger!"

"When will plums be on it?" asked Jan.

"We will have to check the plant until we see little plums," said Dan. "It will be fun to have plump little plums for lunch."

"Plums from plants we planted!" said Jan. "They will be the best plums."

black

blank

blanket

bled

all

time

pack	back	bank	red
back	bank	blank	led
black	blank	blanket	bled

Rags and Dr. Miller

Rags went into the woods with Jan. As they ran along the path, Rags cut her leg on a tin can. The cut bled a lot and had mud on it.

Jan said, "Here, Rags, let me look at your leg. I will try to fix it for you."

Jan picked Rags up and looked at the cut. "That's a bad cut," said Jan. "I will have to get you to Dr. Miller. He is a good animal doctor. He can fix you up."

Jan got a blanket for Rags and rushed to Dr. Miller's house. Dr. Miller wet the cut and got rid of the mud. Then he got a thick pad for it.

"You're a good dog, Rags," said Dr. Miller. "You didn't cry at all."

Then Jan said, "Thank you, Dr. Miller. May Rags go home?"

"Yes," said Dr. Miller, "but she must rest."

Jan set Rags on the blanket and took her home. When Mom looked at Rags resting on the blanket, she said, "Is Rags OK?"

Then Jan had to tell Mom that Rags had cut her leg. "The cut bled a lot so I had to rush Rags to Dr. Miller," said Jan.

"That was good thinking," said Mom. "Let's set Rags in her bed with that blanket."

Rags licked Jan's hand to say thanks.

School in September

On a wet September day, Pam rushed up to Jan after school. "I didn't think I was going to like school," she said. "But I like Ms. Cook. She let me help with her plants today."

"Well, I'm happy I got to be in Mr. Mills's room," said Jan. "He said we will have to get blank tablets for math. I have a black pad at home that will be good."

"We have to get blank tablets for Ms. Cook," said Pam. "I'll have to ask my dad."

The next day in school all the boys and girls had tablets and pens. But when Mr. Mills said he had a math test for them, Jan wasn't happy.

"Oh, no," said Jan to herself, "I don't like tests at all! All the little blanks to fill in!"

But after Mr. Mills handed Jan her test, she felt better. The test was not so bad after all, and she filled in all the blanks.

"What a day!" Pam said when she met Jan after school. "I will not have much time for playing today. I have things to do for school."

Jan said, "After you do school things, we may have time to play."

"I don't think so," said Pam. "I think I will have to do school things all the time."

Time, Time, Time

Time for fun.
Time for play.
Look at the time!
No time today!

No time for this!
No time for that!
No time to sit!
Go get your hat!

But then—
at times,
time's not so rushed.
No,
it's
not.
And then I think,
    "Look
    at
    all
    the
    time
    I've
    got."

clap   clock

class   clop

clip   club

click   cluck

                clutch

(why)   (there)

lap	lip	click	club
clap	clip	clock	cluck
class	click	clop	clutch

Ted

The next day at school, Ms. King said to her class, "This is Ted. He will be in this class with you. Ted, why don't you sit there by Tam?" Then Ms. King helped Ted to his desk. "Ted cannot see," said Ms. King.

Ted had a little black box with him. As Ms. King said things, Ted punched the little box. It went click, click, click.

As class went on, the boys and girls looked at the clock. Then the bell rang. All the boys and girls ran to Ted.

Tam said, "I'm Tam. I sit at the desk next to you."

"I'm Dan," said Dan. "May I ask what the black box is for?"

"Oh, yes," said Ted. "I have to have that just as you have to have tablets. When I punch it, it punches little dots."

Dan began to clap. "That's a good thing you have there," he said.

"Ted," said Tam, "we have a math club here at school. You may be in it, if you like. It's a lot of fun."

"Clubs can be fun," Ted said. "Yes, I think I'll be in the math club. I think I'll like that very much. Thank you."

At Pam's House

Ted was good in math, so Dan asked, "Can you help me with my math after class, Ted?"

"I'll be happy to help," said Ted. "Can you go to my house?"

"Yes," said Dan. "I'll have to go home after class, but I'll be at your house after dinner."

So after dinner Dan went to Ted's house. He rang the bell, and Ted let him in.

They did math for a long time. Then Dan said, "Why don't we rest for a bit. We can go to Pam's house, if you like. Have you met her?"

"No," said Ted. "I think that will be fun."

Ted clutched the little black box in his hands. When they got to Pam's house, Dan rang the bell. Pam let them in.

"Pam," said Dan, "this is Ted. He is in my class."

"Hello," said Pam. Just then the clock rang six times. "Oh, it's six. Little Red will be clucking for her dinner."

Little Red was in her pen back of Pam's house. "Cluck, cluck, cluck!" went the hen.

"She must think I forgot her," said Pam. After Pam had fed Little Red, she said, "Ted, you can pet her, if you wish."

"Thanks," said Ted. "I have not held a hen." Pam picked up Little Red and handed her to Ted. "Oh," said Ted, "she's little."

"Yes," said Pam. "She's a good pet."

Ted held Little Red for a bit. Then he set her in the pen, and he and Pam went back into the house.

Clip-clop! Clip-clop! Clip-clop!

"What is that?" Ted asked. "Is there a horse going by?"

"It is a horse," said Dan. "But it's on Pam's CD player!"

"Oh," said Ted, "I didn't think I was on a ranch!"

slap

slacks

sled

slid

slim

slip

slot

slush

some

led	rim	lap	lot
sled	slim	slap	slot
slid	slip	slacks	slush

At the Letter Box

Kim got up from her desk. "I must get this letter into the letter box," she said. "Will you go with me, Jim?"

"Yes," said Jim. "Maybe we can get my sled when we get back."

They had to get into thick jackets with vests under them. Jim and Kim were very slim, but with the jackets and vests on they didn't look slim at all! They had thick mittens with caps that matched. The slacks and jackets they had on made them look very plump.

Kim tucked the letter into her jacket as they left. "Let's go on the sled," she said.

"OK," said Jim. They hopped on the sled and slid from the top of the hill all the way to the letter box. It was very slushy by the letter box. As Kim got up to slip the letter in the slot, she slipped and fell into the slush.

Jim got up to help her, and then he slipped into the slush. Then as they began to get up, they slid and fell back into the slush.

"Such a mess!" said Jim. "I may just sit here!"

"Some fun!" said Kim. "I may not get this letter in that slot at all!"

Sledding

"Let's all go sledding today," said Tam.

"OK," said Dan. "I'll see if Jim and Kim will go with us."

"We'll go," said Jim and Kim. "We like sledding. Let's get Ted and Pam."

Ted said, "I'll get my sled, and then we can get Pam."

When they got to Pam's house, Pam said, "Yes, I like sledding. Let me get my sled."

They all had on thick jackets and slacks. "If we slip into the slush, we will not get so wet with thick jackets and slacks on," said Kim.

Up to the top of the big hill by Tam's house they went.

Jim and Ted got on Ted's sled, and Dan and Jan got on Jan's sled. Kim, Pam, and Tam all had to fit on Pam's sled. They slid all the way from the top of the big hill. As they got to the end, Dan slipped from the sled into the slush. "Oh!" he yelled. "I got some slush on my slacks and jacket." He got up and began to slap at his slacks to get rid of some of the slush.

The next time they slid from the top of the hill Kim, Pam, and Jim fell into the slush. And the next time it was Ted and Jan who slid from the sleds into the slush. "Some fun," said Jan as she got up and slapped some of the slush from her slacks. "I was in the slush as much as I was on my sled!"

Who Will Go Sledding?

"Let's go sledding today," said Tam.

"OK," said Dan, "and let's ask **??** ."

    Let's ask Kim

    And let's ask **??** .

    Don't forget Ted.

    He has a **??** .

"Is that all?" said Tam to Dan.

"No, I forgot. We must ask **??** ."

flag

flap

flat

flip

flop

one

woman

map	rag	lip	flat
lap	flag	flip	flap
flap	flat	flop	flip

The School Flag

One day Mr. Mills said to his class, "We are going to have a contest. All of you can try to think of a flag for the school. Then Ms. Cook, Ms. King, and I will look at your flags. We will pick the flag we think is the best. And the flag that wins will hang in the classroom of the winner."

On the way home from school that day, Kim said to Jim, "Mom met the woman who made the school flag long ago. Mom was just a little girl when she met her."

"That woman made the flag so long ago," said Jim. "I think she will be sad to see her flag go."

"I don't think she'll be sad. She will help pick the next school flag. "It will be one she likes," said Kim.

The next day all the boys and girls had flags. Ms. King, Mr. Mills, Ms. Cook, and the woman who had made the school flag so long ago looked at all the flags. At last they picked the one that had a red and black school on it. The winner was a girl in Mr. Mills's class.

Mr. Mills said, "I will be happy to have this flag hanging in my classroom."

The woman who made the school flag long ago hugged the girl. Then all the boys and girls looked on as the winner hung her flag in Mr. Mills's room.

After School

That day after school, Jim went up to Tam and Dan. "Let's get bikes and go into the woods on the bike path," Jim said.

"I can't," said Dan. "I have to pick up some things for dinner. Mom will flip if I don't get home and get dinner going."

"Well, why don't you ask?" said Tam.

"I may," said Dan. "You go on. If I can, I'll catch up with you."

So onto the bike path in back of the school Tam and Jim went. After a bit Jim yelled, "Tam, let's rest there by the pond."

"OK," said Tam. "But don't get into all

that mud. There is a better spot by this log."

They sat on the log. Then Jim said, "That math test was a mess! I don't like tests at all."

"But you did so well!" Tam said.

"I can't tell you why," said Jim. "I was thinking I had made the biggest flop of all time."

"Oh, don't think like that," said Tam. "It's not good for you. Let's get going so we can get back for dinner."

They jumped on the bikes and went back up the flat path with jackets flap, flap, flapping in the wind.

"That was fun," said Jim as they went along. "Maybe Dan can go with us next time."

"Maybe so," said Tam.

"Let's go to my mom's shop," Jim said. "We can look at TV in the back room until it's time for Mom to go home. There is a good story on today."

"What is it?" asked Tam.

"It's the story of a woman who hangs by her legs," said Jim. "She can do lots of risky things."

"No, thanks," said Tam. "I don't like to look at things like that on TV."

"Oh, Tam, don't get upset. She has a net under her," said Jim. "And after that she and a little girl do lots of jumps and flips and things on a mat. They're very good at it."

"Oh, OK, I'll look at a little of it with you," said Tam. "But then it's home for supper or my dad will be doing flips!"

A Map

Look at this map.   Can you tell the way
Tam and Jim went?

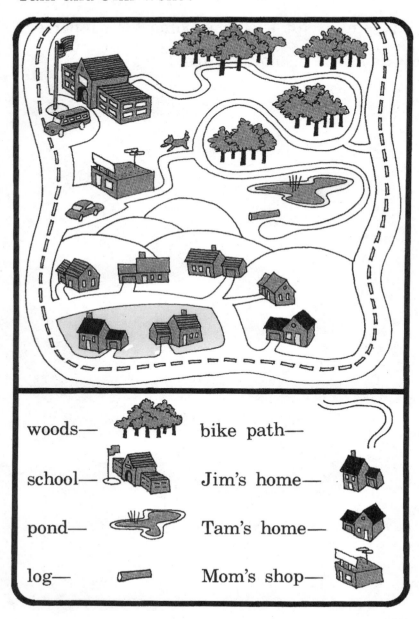

woods—

school—

pond—

log—

bike path—

Jim's home—

Tam's home—

Mom's shop—

spend

spent

speck

spell

(want)   (money)

tank	deck	tell	send
thank	peck	sell	spend
	speck	spell	spent

Ms. King's Gift

The boys and girls in Ms. King's class liked her very much. They wanted to thank her for all the things she did to help them. Tam had a plan.

"Let's get a gift for Ms. King," she said. "Will you help, Dan?"

"All of us can help," he said, "but we will have to get some money."

The next day the class met to think of a good gift for Ms. King. Then they had to think of a way to get money to spend for the gift.

Dan said, "I think I can get some money for the gift. If the rest of you will help me, I can sell some metal junk my mom and dad have. They want me to get rid of it for them."

"That's lucky for us," said Tam. "Will some of you help me pick the best gift we can get?"

So some of the boys and girls in the class met with Tam. Some of them went with Dan to try to sell the junk.

"I think a plant for Ms. King's desk is a good gift," said Tam. "We can get one at Mrs. Benton's shop. She has some plants."

"Yes," said one of the boys, "a plant's a very good gift. Can we go after school one day?"

"Yes," said Tam. "When we get the money, we can all go."

The next day, when Dan and the rest got back, they said, "We have the money. We want to help spend it."

So after school, the class went to Mrs. Benton's shop. She had lots of plants for them to see. They picked a little plant in a red pot.

Dan handed Mrs. Benton the money for the plant. Mrs. Benton thanked the class. "Ms. King is lucky to have such a good class," she said.

Dan said, "We have a little money left to spend. Let's get a ribbon for the plant so it will look better."

The boys and girls had the plant on Ms. King's desk the next day. "Oh, what a good gift," she said. "You have made me very happy. Thank you."

Spelling, Plants, and Bugs

Dan and Pam were at Pam's house. Pam was picking bugs from the plants on the windowsills. Dan looked upset.

"When are we going to do spelling?" Dan asked.

"Dan," said Pam, "my plants are sick. See this one? It just flops. And all the buds fell from this one. I have to get rid of the bugs."

Dan said, "Did you forget, Pam? We're going to have a spelling test. I spent all day on this list. I haven't got it yet."

"Oh, you'll get it," said Pam. "You can spell. You're a good speller, Dan." She went on, "I'm going to help you. But you don't want the bugs to kill my plants, do you? I had one plant killed by bugs."

"What do the bugs look like?" Dan asked.

"They look like little black specks," said Pam, picking a speck from one of the plants. Then she said, "There is a saying I think you'll like, Dan."

"Oh," said Dan, "what is it?"

"Sometimes," said Pam, "the best way to get help is by helping."

Then Dan said, "OK, Pam, I get it. May I help pick bugs from your plant?"

"Why, Dan," said Pam, "I didn't think you were going to ask!"

"I may not be so good at spelling," said Dan, "but I'm very good at getting a hint."

spin

spill

spun

sell	run	pen	pet
spell	sun	pin	pot
spill	spun	spin	spot

The Puppy and the Top

Pam was looking at the doll she got from Grandma and Grandpa. Gus said to them, "You didn't have to spend so much!"

"Oh, we didn't spend that much," said Grandma. "We made the doll's things."

"Here is a little something I got for you," said Grandpa to Pam. "It's a black top with red spots. When you spin it fast, the spots look like a ribbon."

Chester, the puppy, ran past as Grandpa spun the top. Chester began to hit it. When the top did not spin so fast, the red specks did not look like a red ribbon.

At last the top fell and hit Chester. He ran and hid.

Grandpa said to Pam, "Your puppy didn't like that. You had better get him. I think he's one unhappy little dog."

"I'll look for him," Pam said. She looked under her desk. "Here he is!" she yelled. "I've got him."

Pam picked up her puppy and patted him. Chester was happy to be back with Pam.

The Inky Puppy

When Pam went to school, her puppy got into her bedroom. He jumped from the bed to the desk. When he landed, he hit the ink on the desk. The ink began to spill on the rug. It made a big red spot.

At lunchtime Pam went to her room to get her spelling book. "Oh, no!" she yelled. "Look at this mess!"

Gus ran to look.

Pam said, "Look what that puppy did! He spilled ink on my rug."

"Well," said Gus, "you did not shut him in the kitchen when you left for school. You must do that when you are going to be away."

Just then Pam's puppy ran past them. He had ink spots on him.

"My, but that's an inky puppy!" Gus said to Pam.

"Here, Inky! Here, Inky!" said Pam.

Chester ran to Pam, and she did a good job on his ink spots with some suds and a rag. At last the puppy had no ink spots left on him. From then on, he always ran to Pam when she said, "Here, Inky!"

You Can Do This

blank	must	eggs	pack
ink	tablet	nuts	lamp
ask	camp	vest	on

1. animal	2. dig	3. run	4. ??
book	??	spin	bet
??	fill	??	cup
duck	get	under	dish
end	hit	very	end

5. like	6. sun	7. jet	8. gas
??	top	kiss	hand
next	up	??	??
or	??	man	just
plant	want	nest	kitchen

stand

stack

stem

step

ham hem stem	band sand stand	sick sack stack	stand stem step

What Can We Do?

One day after school Jan, Jim, and Kim sat on the steps. "Let's get our bikes and take off. We can be back by dinner," said Jan.

"OK," said Kim, "that's better than just standing here."

But Kim had forgotten that her bike had to be fixed. "So, what can we do?" she asked.

"Oh, Kim, there are lots of things to do," said Jim. "We'll just have to think."

"OK," said Kim, "I'll try to think of something."

"We can go to the pond and catch fish," said Jan.

"It's all muddy by the pond. I don't like to step in mud," said Kim. "And I will not stand in that mess just to catch a fish."

"OK," said Jim, "let's go look at TV then."

"Oh, I don't want to look at TV. We look at TV all the time!" said Kim.

"You don't want to look at TV. You can't go on your bike. You don't want to step in mud by the pond. What do you want to do?" yelled Jim.

"OK," said Kim, "there is a stack of books at our house. We can go look at some good books."

"Good," said Jan, "maybe you'll have a book in that stack that is filled with things to do!"

Lots of Stems

When Dan got home from school one day, a big stack of books was in the kitchen. He went to Jan, who was standing in her room. "Why is that big stack of plant books in the kitchen?" he asked.

"I have to take them to school," said Jan. "I wanted to see what the stems are like on lots of plants. All the kids in my class are going to look at the books."

Jan picked up one of the books. "Look at this plant," she said. "It has such a thick stem that it will stand up all by itself."

She set that book by the stack and picked up the next one. "Look at this plant. It has a thin stem," she said. "It can't stand up by itself."

She picked up the next book in the stack. "Look at the stem on this plant," she said. "If you pinch it on the end, it will get lots of little stems. I think I like this one best."

"Can that plant be kept in homes?" asked Dan.

"I think so," said Jan. "Maybe I'll get some houseplants for my room. I can pick what I want from the books. I'll have to look for a good plant shop. I may end up with a room filled with plants!"

Let's Look It Up

One Step at a Time. 6

The Lucky Fox 14

Good-by, Mr. Mills 22

Back on the Job 36

Time After Time 47

Off the Top 53

The Last Stand 65

Going Our Way 78

stiff

stick

still

stitch

sting

stop

stuck

stem	sick	patch	sill
step	stick	pitch	still
stop	stuck	stitch	stiff

55

At Peg's Plant Shop

The next day Jan asked Ted and Dan to go to Peg's Plant Shop with her. "We can stop on our way home from school," said Jan.

"I'll go," said Ted. "Why don't you ask Tam? I think she likes houseplants. She has lots of them at her house."

"OK," said Jan. "I'll see if she wants to go along."

When Jan asked her, Tam said, "Oh, yes, I'd like to go. That's much better than being stuck in the house. There's a stiff wind, so we'd better get our jackets."

Peg's Plant Shop was little, but it had lots of plants. There were plants with stiff thick stems and plants with thin stems. There were big plants and little plants. One plant looked just like a bunch of little sticks. Some of the plants had buds.

There was one plant with little red buds. "Oh, I want that one," said Jan.

"That's a good houseplant," said Peg, the woman in the shop. "But the little stiff things can stick you."

"Oh, no!" said Ted. "I'm stuck! Did that plant sting me?"

"Yes," said Jan. "It's stuck in your jacket. It made a little rip, but a stitch will fix it up. You'll be OK."

"Well," said Ted, "you got a plant, and I got stuck!"

Good Luck for Pam

On the way home from Peg's Plant Shop, Jan, Tam, and Ted passed Pam's house. Pam was up on one rung of a stepladder picking plums. She had the last big plum by the stem as Jan, Tam, and Ted were passing by.

Tam stopped and looked up at Pam. "Pam!" she yelled. "There's a big bug on your neck. Stand still, or it will sting you!"

Pam slapped at the bug, and the ladder began to slip. "Stand still!" yelled Tam. She rushed to the ladder and held it. All the plums spilled from Pam's basket.

Tam helped Pam from the ladder and picked up the plums. "That was a bad spot to be in," said Tam. "Did that bug sting you?"

Pam felt her neck. "No," she said, "I don't think so. I was lucky I did not slip off that stepladder. Here, Tam, take some plums."

"Oh, thanks, Pam," said Tam. "Dad and I can cook up some plum jam. He likes that a lot."

"That's good," said Pam. "This ended up to be a good day for us. That bug didn't sting me, and you will have some good plum jam."

They Say "Stop"

skin

skip

skunk

how

grandmother

lip	tin	bunk	skip
dip	win	junk	skin
skip	skin	skunk	skunk

The Pet Shop

Mr. Sancho stood in his pet shop and looked at the boys and girls going to school. It was such a wet day they didn't run or skip. They all looked so sad.

"What a day!" Mr. Sancho said to himself. "No one will come in here to get a pet." So he fed the dogs and the fish in the tanks. He fed the kittens. The little skunk was very still in her box.

Mr. Sancho said, "The boys and girls will look at the skunk. They will like it. But moms and dads don't want skunks for pets. Grandmothers and grandfathers get them for boys and girls. I must get grandmothers and grandfathers to come into my shop. They will like the skunk. Then I can sell it to one of them."

The next day Mr. Sancho set up a big jug for the boys and girls to see. On the jug was a tag:

> Grandmothers! Grandfathers!
> You can win a pet if you can tell how much money is in this jug.

Next to the jug and the tag was the skunk in her box.

The next day the boys and girls going to school passed Mr. Sancho's shop and looked at the tag. Grandmothers and grandfathers did come into the shop. Pam's grandmother did not tell how much money was in the jug, but she did like the little tan puppy. Tam's grandfather did not tell how much money was in the jug, but he did get six fish from the tank for Tam.

Tam said, "I like that fish with the pink skin best."

Her grandfather said, "Here, Tam. The fish are for you. But don't run or skip with them."

When they left, Mr. Sancho said to himself, "I can sell some of my pets, but no one wants the skunk. And no one took that little kitten. No one can tell me how much money is in the jug. I think the little skunk and the kitten like me. Maybe I will not sell them after all!"

swam

swim

swing

would

him Kim swim	ham jam swam	ring sing swing	swim swam swing

Swing or Swim?

Linda Fisher is a girl in Pam's room at school. One day Linda's mother said to Linda, "I would like to get something for you. I can get a pool for you to swim in, or I can get a set of swings. But you must pick one. We don't have room in back of the house for the swings and a pool. And I don't have that much money to spend. So you can think and then tell me what you want."

At school that day, Linda said to Pam, "My mother said she would get me a swing or a pool to swim in. But I must pick one. Do you think the pool is better? Or would you pick the swing?"

"Well," said Pam, "I think a swing is better. I have a little pond by my house, so I can swim there. I swam there a lot last summer. If you get the swing, we can have lots of fun this summer. You can come to my house to swim. And I can go to your house to swing."

"That's what I'll pick," said Linda. "That way I get a spot to swim, a set of swings, and a pal!"

Picking a Swing

The next day after school, Linda said to her mother, "I think I would like to have the swing set. Pam Sands said I can swim in the pond by her house this summer. If I have a swing, she can come here to swing, and on hot days, I can go there to swim."

"OK," said Ms. Fisher. "We can look at swings at Mr. Dennis's shop. He has a lot of swing sets to pick from. I'll pick you up from school on my way home. We can go from there."

"Oh, good," said Linda. "It will not be long till the days are hot and sunny. Then we can swing all day long!"

"Well, maybe not that long!" said Ms. Fisher. "But you will have a good summer."

When she got to school that day, Linda ran to tell Pam that she was going to get a swing set. "Mom and I are going to pick the swing today after school," said Linda.

"May I see it when you get it set up?" asked Pam.

"Oh, yes," said Linda. "Then this summer we can swing and swim all the time."

That day Linda and Ms. Fisher went to Mr. Dennis's shop. There were lots of swings to pick from. Linda picked a red one.

Ms. Fisher asked, "Will you take a check, Mr. Dennis?"

"Yes," said Mr. Dennis. "You can't get the swing home by yourself, Ms. Fisher. I have a man and a woman who can take it on a van. They will set it up for you."

"That's good of you, Mr. Dennis," said Ms. Fisher.

"That's just what made this a good shop," said Mr. Dennis. "If you are happy with what you get here, maybe you'll come back."

"I will, Mr. Dennis!" said Linda. "I like to come here!"

twig

twist

twin

where

deer

dig	fist	twig	twin
wig	list	twist	twig
twig	twist	twin	twist

A Pet in the Woods

On one of the last winter days, Mr. Benton and the twins went to visit a woman and a man who had a house in the woods. Pat and Jack Speck were very happy to see them.

Pat said to them, "I have a pet who comes from the woods to see me. I fed her one day and she has always come back. Animals can't get much in the winter woods."

"I'd like to see her," said Kim. "Where is she?"

"She's in the woods," said Jack. "The visitor is a little tan deer. She looks like Bambi. If you want to see her, we'll have to go into the woods."

"Well, let's get some jackets on and get going," said Pat.

As they went along the path, Jim looked for the deer. He looked at a nest made of twigs.

"Do deer like twigs?" he asked.

"Well, I fed her some tender twigs and dry grass," said Jack, "and she liked them."

"Then I'll twist off a twig for her lunch," said Jim.

After some time Pat said, "I can't think where my little deer is today. Maybe we'd better go back home."

When they got back, Jim and Kim said, "Thank you, Pat and Jack. We liked the trip into the woods. Maybe we will have better luck next time and get to see your deer."

A Log Cabin

"I have to make a log cabin for school, Kim. Let's get twigs from the woods and cut them to make little logs. My dad will let us make the cabin in the kitchen. Will you help me?" asked Pam.

"Yes, it will be fun to help. Chester can go with us," said Kim.

Kim and Pam went into the woods with Pam's puppy, Chester, and picked up twigs. They did not want twigs with buds on them. They wanted dry twigs ten inches long. Chester left the path, but he kept running back with twigs for them.

Pam looked at twigs on some big plants. "Let's twist this twig until it comes off the plant," she said. They twisted and twisted.

The twig left the plant with a snap! Kim fell back!

"Are you OK?" Pam asked.

"Yes," said Kim, getting up. "But where is Chester? Has he left us? Where can he be?"

"Let's look for him," said Pam.

Up the twisting path they ran and ran. At last, there was Chester. Good Chester! He had a bunch of twigs, and he stood wagging and wagging.

"Chester is such a good puppy," said Pam. "He got a lot of twigs for us. Do you think he wants to help us make the log cabin?"

You Can Do It

duck	jacket	supper
pig	pants	lunch
kiss	hat	cluck
deer	twig	dinner
figs	bathroom	chicken
ship	bedroom	slacks
bus	contest	hatch
jet	kitchen	egg
red	clock	animal
big	yams	money
black	tick	cash
pink	time	check

crack

crash

crab

crisp

crust

crush

about

cash	crash	sack	crab
mash	crush	crack	crust
crash	crust	crab	crisp

To Catch a Crab

Jan was sitting on her bed with a book for school. She had to tell her class about crabs and crabbing. "There is a lot to think about," she said to herself. "I think someday I'll go crabbing myself."

Here is what Jan said in class about crabbing.

Crabbing can be fun. In a lot of ways, it is like fishing. You can catch a crab if you try.

Just sit on a dock with a little rod. You will have to have bits of chicken. Crabs like chicken. The chicken must be on a little hook. Let it hang where a crab can get it. Then snap up on the rod, and if you are lucky, you will catch a crab!

Crabs have shells. So after you catch a crab, the shell will have to be cracked. To crack the shell, you must cook the crab. Then when the shell is still hot, crush the shell with a little hammer or something.

Sometimes crab is crushed into little bits, and then it can be fixed with a crisp crust. That is so good!

I think it would be fun for our class to go crabbing someday. Then if we catch some crabs, we can cook them and have a big crab dinner!

May I Help?

Dan ran into the kitchen one day after school. "May I help with dinner?" he asked.

Mrs. Bell said, "Oh, my goodness, yes! Thank you, Dan. The Bentons will be here for dinner. I have cooked the crab, but will you crack some nuts? Get the nutcracker in that cabinet. We can snack on the nuts until dinner."

Dan got the nutcracker from the cabinet. Then he sat on a bench in the kitchen and began to crack the nuts. Oh, but what a mess he made! He spilled some shells on the mat under the bench. Then when he bent to get the dustpan, he upset the bag of nuts. The nuts fell into the trash can. And when he bent to get the nuts from the trash can, the trash can fell with a crash, and all the trash spilled.

"What a mess!" said Dan.

"That's OK," said his mother. "Why don't you let me fix things up here, and you can fix up the bathroom."

"OK, I may be better at that," said Dan. "I just want to help."

"You can help, and you do," said Mrs. Bell.

So Dan got a mop and a rag and went to fix up the bathroom. He filled a pan in the sink. When he stuck the rag in the pan, the mop fell and the pan spilled. "Oh, no!" said Dan. "I've made a mess of the bathroom!"

He mopped up the spill and went back to

the kitchen. "I just wanted to help, but I made a mess of the bathroom and the kitchen," he said.

"Oh, Dan, don't let that upset you," said his mother. "We all have bad days. Here, have some milk and crackers. We will try to make this a better day for you. The Bentons will be here for dinner!"

Fred

Frank

frog

handle

log	bank	led	thank
fog	sank	red	Frank
frog	Frank	Fred	frog

Catching a Frog

Frank and Fred go to school with Jan. One day Frank said to Fred, "Let's go to the pond and try to catch a frog."

"OK," said Fred. So off they went.

They sat by the pond to begin looking for frogs. Just then one big frog hopped past Frank and jumped into the pond.

"Oh, no! We missed it!" said Fred.

"Just sit still," Frank said. "I'll bet it will just swim a little bit and then come up here and sit in the mud."

Just then a bigger frog jumped into the pond.

"Oh, we missed that frog!" Fred yelled.

"Look! There's one on that log! See where that little twig is sticking up? The frog is trying to catch some bugs. Oh, it got a bug! Did you see that?"

"Look at that big frog!" said Frank. "It must be ten inches long!"

"Look! A frog jumped into our net. I think we can get it if we grab the net fast."

Fred held the wooden handle and lifted the net. Then a twig cracked. Just as the frog jumped, Fred twisted the handle and flipped the net.

"Wow! We got it! We got that big frog!" said Frank. "Do you think we could get it home in the net?"

"No, we'll have to get a bucket or maybe a box with a lid, or it will get away," Fred said.

Fred ran home to get a box. When he went back, Jan went with him.

"Look at the back legs on that frog," she said. "It will never stay on the bottom of that box!"

"Well, if there is a lid on it, the frog can't get away," said Frank. "Now we'll have to get it some bugs."

Jan went to look for some bugs. Frank and Fred lifted the net and the frog into the box and set the lid on it.

"Is the frog OK?" asked Fred.

"I can't tell. We'll have to bend the lid back so we can see it."

They bent the lid back just a little until they could see the frog.

"I don't think this frog wants to be in this box. It's just sitting there. It wants to swim, sit in the mud, and catch bugs. Could we let it go?" asked Fred.

"Yes, it's a very unhappy frog," said Frank as he lifted the lid off the box. The frog jumped up and hopped back into the pond.

Jan ran back to the boys. "I could not catch one little bug," she said sadly.

"That's OK," said Frank. "We let the frog go. It wasn't happy, and we like looking at frogs in ponds better than looking at frogs in boxes."

Look It Up

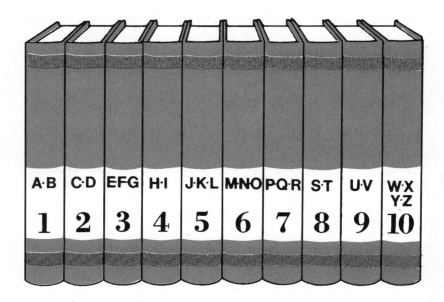

Look at the books. Then tell the number of the book you must get if you want to look up something.

dogs	frogs	the <u>sun</u>
cats	bats	the <u>wind</u>
maps	pigs	how to make <u>ink</u>
fish	horses	how we got <u>numbers</u>
jets	skunks	how we get <u>milk</u>
rocks	bikes	

drop

drip

drink

dress

drum

cold

nose

mess	sink	mop	gum
less	think	drop	hum
dress	drink	drip	drum

Not a Drop To Drink

Rags sat next to her pan. She had sipped and sipped until her pan was dry. There was no one at home to fill her pan for her, and she wanted a drink.

Rags sat and looked at the kitchen sink. Drip, drip, drip, but not one drop in her pan. Oh, how she wanted just one little sip!

A little bit of milk was left in Nat's pan. Rags lapped at the milk. It was not very good, but she did want a drink!

So Rags had a drink of Nat's milk, and then she took a nap.

Nat ran into the kitchen to get the rest of his milk. But there was no milk! He looked at Rags and went back to his mat.

When Jan got home, she filled Nat's pan with milk. She filled Rags's pan from the sink. She said to herself, "We must get this sink fixed. It has dripped and dripped for days."

Nat and Rags had good drinks from the pans. "What good pets!" said Jan. "This dripping sink must make you want to drink a lot."

Rags sat next to Nat's pan after her pan was dry. "Do you like milk?" asked Jan. "Maybe Nat will let you sip his milk." At that, Nat hissed.

A Wet Day at Home

Kim sat up in bed looking sad. Her puppy, Sandy, was on the bed with her.

"Sandy," she said sadly, "I wish I didn't have to miss school. We're going to have a test today, and I'm going to miss it. I can't go to school with this cold."

Kim looked at a big drop on the window. It was a wet, cold day, and she had to stay in bed.

Just then her father looked into her room. "How are you?" he asked. "I'm going to stay home with you today. Here, I've got some nose drops and cold pills for you. They should help."

"I wish I felt better," said Kim. "I must get back to school, but I can't go if my nose drips all the time."

Mr. Benton said, "Well, we'll see how you are after you have the nose drops and the pills. Now drink this with your pill and try to nap until lunchtime. If you rest it should help get rid of that cold."

"OK," said Kim. "Maybe Sandy will have a nap with me." Sandy just licked Kim's hand.

By lunchtime Kim had had her nap and felt better. Dad cooked lunch for them and took it to Kim's room on a tray.

"This isn't so bad," said Kim. "Thanks for cooking lunch, Dad. A hot lunch is so good on a cold day. May I let Sandy have a little?"

"OK," said Dad. "He's a good little puppy today. Then after you've had your next pill, why don't you get dressed? I think you are much better."

Kim got up to dress. She took her pill and her nose drops. Then she went to the window. "It's still so wet," she said as she looked at the big drops on the glass. "I'll have to stay in all day."

"Colds can get to you," said her dad. "But there's a lot you can do. You can do your math and spelling for school or play your drums. You can help me get dinner."

"It isn't so bad to be home with this cold," said Kim. "It's fun to be here with you and Sandy."

Kim and her dad hugged, and Sandy wagged and wagged.

bring

brick

bran

brand

sick	can	king	ran
click	man	sing	bran
brick	bran	bring	brand

Linda's Gift

"Did you bring home a box of bran when you went shopping?" Linda asked Ted one day.

"No, we don't get bran. We get the brand of corn crisps that puff up in milk. When you send in some money and the box tops from corn crisps, you can get books or other gifts. You have to check what you want on the list on the back of the box," said Ted.

"Well," said Linda, "I don't like corn crisps. I like bran. Maybe I can get them to send gifts for bran box tops."

So Linda cut the top from a box of bran. She sent the box top and a letter to the address on the box. Ted helped with the letter.

In the letter Linda said, "You don't send gifts to children who send in your box tops. I may stop getting bran and begin getting corn crisps."

In just six days Linda got a letter and a box. There was a book about animals in the box. The letter said

Ms. Fisher,

Thank you for your letter and the box top. We are glad to send you this book.

From now on, every box of bran will have a list of things children can get by sending in bran box tops. This may help us to sell lots of bran.

Linda was glad she had sent the letter. She liked bran much better than corn crisps.

A House for Sandy

Sandy, Kim's pup, was getting bigger every day. He slept on Kim's bed. But her mother and father weren't at all happy about it.

One day Mom said to Kim, "Sandy is getting to be such a big dog. I think he should have a bed and house for himself. Maybe you, your dad, and I can think of something."

Kim went to look for her father. "Mom thinks we should fix up a house for Sandy. What do you think?" she asked.

"Well," her father began, "I can bring home some plans for doghouses. Then we can look at them and see if we can come up with a good one for Sandy."

The next day they all sat in the kitchen and looked at lots of plans for doghouses.

Dad said, "There are lots of good-looking doghouses in this book. I think we should make Sandy's house from brick, like this one."

"A brick doghouse!" said Mother. "What about the money? It would take a lot of money for a brick doghouse."

"Oh, Mom," Kim begged, "this house will be good for Sandy. It will last a long time, and Sandy will not have to spend so much time in my room."

At last, Mom said a brick doghouse would be OK.

So Kim and her father got lots of bricks and began Sandy's house. "This will be the best doghouse on the block," said Kim.

For days Kim and her father spent a lot of time on Sandy's house. Kim's dad said, "Your mother will like Sandy's house when she sees it."

"I think so," said Kim. "But will Sandy like it? I'm going to miss him in my room with me all the time."

"Oh," said her father, "you can still bring him in sometimes."

At last, the house was all made. It was red brick with a little brick path going up to it. Kim yelled for Sandy. Sandy sniffed at the house and then went into it.

"He likes it!" said Kim. "It's the best house ever made for the best dog ever."

track

trick

truck

trunk

sick	back	duck	bunk
lick	pack	luck	skunk
trick	track	truck	trunk

Planning a Trip

Manny is a boy in Dan and Jan's school. One day Manny's dad said to him, "How would you like to take a trip? Just you and I could go, if you think you'd like that."

"Where would we go?" asked Manny.

"How about to a ranch in the West?" said his dad.

"But I can't miss school," said Manny. "I could never catch up if we were away for long."

"Oh, we would go in the summer when you are not in school," his dad said.

"I think that would be fun," said Manny.

"Good," said his dad. "We will go in my

truck so we can pack a big trunk with our things and stay for a good, long time. We will have lots of plans to make for the trip, but we have time to plan."

"We will have to pick spots to stop on the way," said Manny. "That can be lots of fun. We have to think about how long to stay."

"You've never ridden a horse, have you, Manny?" asked his dad.

"No, but I'm willing to try," said Manny. "I've never had a trip like this. I wish we could go now."

"Well, if we plan a little every day, the time will pass faster. Then before you can think, summer will be here, and we'll be on our way. But now you must get dressed and be on your way to school."

Dan ran up to Manny on the way home from school that day. Manny told him about the trip his dad and he were planning.

"What a trip!" said Dan. "Maybe I can help you with the plans."

"I wish you could help me pass the time until we go!" said Manny. "Planning the trip will be fun, but I want to be going. I want to be there—now!"

Lucky, the Ranch Horse

When Dan got home that day, he went to look at TV. The story on TV made him think of Manny and his trip. This is the story that was on TV.

Lucky was a big horse. He was the fastest runner on Bell Ranch. He belonged to Ms. Bellman. He was such a fast runner that Ms. Bellman had a track made for him. Every day Ms. Bellman took Lucky to the track on the Bell Ranch truck.

One day they went to the track, but Lucky didn't want to run. Ed, a man who helped at the track, began to saddle Lucky. The horse was mad! He was pitching and bucking. Ed held on to him.

"We must think of a trick to get the saddle on him," Ed said. "I can't handle him when he's like this!"

"I've got it!" said Ms. Bellman. Then she ran to the truck. When she got back, she had Lucky's lunch. Lucky liked the lunch so much he stopped bucking. Then he had a drink.

By that time, Ed had the saddle on Lucky and was up on his back. He was trying to get Lucky to run. The big horse ran, but he didn't run very fast.

"It was the lunch that did it," Ed told Ms. Bellman.

"Then we must not let him have lunch until he has run," Ms. Bellman said. "It's not good for him."

"But how will we get the saddle on him?"
Ed asked.

"Oh, we will think of another way to do it,"
said Ms. Bellman. "We will think of a good
trick for next time."

Then Dan said to himself, "I can't think of
the trick they will play on Lucky. I will have
to look at TV next Sunday. Then I will tell
Manny the rest of the story."

TO THE TEACHER

The MERRILL READING PROGRAM consists of eight Readers developed on linguistic principles applicable to the teaching of reading. The rationale of the program and detailed teaching procedures are described in the Teacher's Edition of each Reader.

All words introduced in this Reader are listed on the following pages under the headings "Words in Pattern," "Sight Words," and "Applications of Patterning."

Words listed as "Words in Pattern" represent additional matrices in the first major set of spelling patterns. Consonant-letter combinations in initial position are a common element in the pattern words of this Reader. Fifteen initial consonant-letter combinations are introduced: *pl, bl, cl, sl, fl, sp, st, sk, sw, tw, cr, fr, dr, br,* and *tr*. In addition, words having consonant-letter combinations in both initial and final positions are presented. New final consonant-letter combinations in the words of this Reader are *ff* and *sp*.

Words listed as "Sight Words" are high-frequency words introduced to provide normal sentence patterns in the stories.

Words listed as "Applications of Patterning" include new words based on patterns and sight words previously introduced, combinations of words (compound words), additional tense forms, plurals, possessives, and contractions.

WORD LISTS FOR TEACHER REFERENCE

Pages	Words in Pattern	Sight Words
Unit 1 5-10	plan plant plum plump	what
Unit 2 11-16	black blank blanket bled	all time
Unit 3 17-22	clap class clip click clock clop club cluck clutch	why there
Unit 4 23-28	slap slacks sled slid slim slip slot slush	some

Pages	Words in Pattern	Sight Words
Unit 5 29-36	flag flap flat flip flop	one woman
Unit 6 37-42	spend spent speck spell	want money
Unit 7 43-48	spin spill spun	
Unit 8 49-54	stand stack stem step	take off our
Unit 9 55-60	stiff stick still stitch sting stop stuck	
Unit 10 61-64	skin skip skunk	how grandmother

Pages	Words in Pattern	Sight Words	Pages	Words in Pattern	Sight Words
Unit 11 65-70	swam swim swing	would	Unit 15 89-94	drop drip drink dress drum	cold nose
Unit 12 71-76	twig twist twin	where deer			
Unit 13 77-82	crack crash crab crisp crust crush	about	Unit 16 95-100	bring brick bran brand	
Unit 14 83-88	Fred Frank frog	handle	Unit 17 101-107	track trick truck trunk	

Applications of Patterning

(The underlined numbers are page numbers.)

Unit 1	Unit 3	Unit 6	Unit 8
5-10	**17-22 cont.**	**37-42**	**49-54 cont.**

Unit 1
5-10

bigger
digging
getting
hugged
planted
plants
plums
rushed
sunny
way

Unit 2
11-16

animal
blanks
cry
Miller
Miller's
oh
resting
say
times
time's
try
you're

Unit 3
17-22

clubs
clucking
clutched
hello
player
punched

Unit 3
17-22 cont.

punches
she's
Ted
Ted's

Unit 4
23-28

letter
matched
mittens
slapped
sledding
sleds
slipped
slushy

Unit 5
29-36

ago
biggest
classroom
contest
doing
flags
flapping
flips
hanging
hangs
risky
she'll
supper
they're
upset
winner

Unit 6
37-42

buds
flops
haven't
hint
kill
killed
lucky
metal
plant's
saying
sometimes
specks
speller
spelling
thanked
wanted
windowsills

Unit 7
43-48

always
egg
inky
landed
lunchtime
patted
something
spilled
unhappy

Unit 8
49-54

forgotten
homes
houseplants
itself

Unit 8
49-54 cont.

muddy
standing
stems
steps

Unit 9
55-60

basket
ended
houseplant
Peg's
stepladder
sticks
stopped
there's
wants
we'd

Unit 10
61-64

come
grandfathers
grandmothers
himself
kittens
Sancho
Sancho's
skunks
stood
tanks

Unit 11
65-70

days
Dennis
Dennis's

Applications of Patterning

(The underlined numbers are page numbers.)

Unit 11 **65-70** cont.	Unit 13 **77-82**	Unit 15 **89-94**	Unit 16 **95-100** cont.
Fisher	cabinet	colds	gifts
Linda	crabbing	cooking	glad
Linda's	crabs	dressed	other
mother	cracked	drinks	plans
pal	crackers	dripped	puff
pool	crushed	dripping	Sandy's
summer	dock	drips	sending
swings	dustpan	drops	slept
yourself	goodness	drums	sniffed
	hammer	father	weren't
	nutcracker	glass	
	snack	hissed	
Unit 12 **71-76**	someday	lapped	Unit 17 **101-107**
	trash	Sandy	
animals		should	another
Bambi	Unit 14 **83-88**	sipped	before
cabin		tray	Bellman
comes	bottom	wagged	belonged
dry	boxes	window	bucking
grass	bucket	you've	Ed
I'd	catching		faster
inches	could	Unit 16 **95-100**	fastest
make	flipped		Lucky's
snap	frogs	address	Manny
tender	grab	block	Manny's
twigs	never	bricks	pitching
twins	now	children	planning
twisted	ponds	corn	ridden
twisting	sadly	crisps	runner
visit	stay	doghouse	saddle
visitor	sticking	doghouses	Sunday
wagging	trying	ever	told
winter	wow	every	willing
			you'd